Anxiety RX

Coping Mechanisms

Developing Effective Strategies for Managing Anxiety

Matthew Hoover

Table of the Contents:

Chapter 1: Introduction

In the world we live in today, it is nearly impossible not to experience anxiety at some point. The hustle and bustle of modern life, filled with incessant demands and a never-ending stream of information, can make even the calmest person feel overwhelmed and anxious. It is completely normal to feel anxiety in certain situations. It is our body's natural response to stress, an alarm that goes off when we feel threatened, under pressure, or are facing a challenging situation.

However, for some individuals, anxiety goes beyond these normal sensations of nervousness. It is not just a fleeting feeling or a reasonable response to a stressful situation, but a constant companion that does not go away, even when the situation improves. It can interfere with daily activities, job performance, and relationships. It can cause distress that is out of proportion to the triggering situation. In this case, we are talking about an anxiety disorder, which is a serious mental health problem that affects millions of people around the globe.

The purpose of this book, "Anxiety RX," is to offer a comprehensive guide on understanding, managing, and treating anxiety. Throughout the following chapters, we will delve into what anxiety is, exploring its causes, symptoms, and the science behind it. We will discuss various treatment options available, with a specific emphasis on medication (RX), and guide you through different therapeutic approaches that have proven effective in managing anxiety disorders. Additionally, we will provide helpful strategies for self-help and discuss the role of lifestyle choices in managing anxiety.

This book is meant to serve as a valuable resource for anyone dealing with anxiety themselves or anyone who knows someone suffering from it. It aims to foster a better understanding and offer hope and guidance for those who might feel lost amidst the turmoil of this mental health condition.

Anxiety can be a debilitating condition, but it is also treatable. Many people with anxiety disorders live fulfilling, productive lives. The first step towards getting better is understanding what you're dealing with, and that's what we hope to provide in this book. The journey might seem challenging, but remember, you are not alone. Let's begin this journey towards understanding and managing anxiety together.

Chapter 2: Understanding Anxiety

Anxiety, in its most basic form, is the body's natural response to stress. It's a feeling of fear or apprehension about what's to come. You might experience it before a big event, a job interview, or when facing a problem at work or in personal life. This is 'normal' anxiety, an inherent part of our evolutionary survival mechanism known as the 'fight-or-flight' response, which prepares our bodies to respond to perceived threats.

However, when these feelings of anxiety persist and become chronic, they can take a more serious form, known as anxiety disorders. These disorders go beyond the occasional worry or fear. For a person with an anxiety disorder, the anxiety does not go away and can get worse over time, often interfering with daily activities such as job performance, school work, and relationships.

There are several types of anxiety disorders, including generalized anxiety disorder (GAD), panic disorder, and various phobia-related disorders. Let's delve a little deeper into each of these:

1. **Generalized Anxiety Disorder (GAD)**: This is characterized by chronic anxiety, exaggerated worry, and tension, even when there is little or nothing to provoke it.
2. **Panic Disorder**: People with this condition have feelings of terror that strike suddenly and repeatedly without warning. Other symptoms of a panic attack

include sweating, chest pain, palpitations (unusually strong or irregular heartbeats), and a feeling of choking, which can make the person feel like they're having a heart attack or "going crazy."

3. **Phobia-related Disorders**: A phobia is an intense fear of—or aversion to—specific things or situations. Although it can be any object, place, or situation, certain experiences or topics are more common, such as fear of flying (aviophobia), fear of spiders (arachnophobia), or fear of heights (acrophobia).

4. **Specific Phobias**: A specific phobia is an excessive and persistent fear related to a specific object, situation, or activity. These can range widely from fear of particular animals, like snakes or spiders, to fear of certain environments, like heights or enclosed spaces. Individuals with specific phobias will often go to great lengths to avoid what they fear, or they endure it with great distress, impacting their quality of life.

5. **Agoraphobia**: Once thought to be a type of panic disorder, agoraphobia is now recognized as a separate anxiety disorder. It is characterized by a fear of being in places or situations where escape might be difficult or help unavailable should a panic attack occur. It often leads to avoidance of public places and can, in extreme cases, result in the person not leaving their home.

6. **Separation Anxiety Disorder**: Often thought of as something that only children deal with, separation anxiety can also affect adults. It's characterized by a fear

of being apart from people to whom the individual is attached. The fear is beyond what is appropriate for the person's age, causes distress, and often impacts their ability to function.

7. **Selective Mutism**: This is a somewhat rare disorder, usually seen in children, characterized by a consistent failure to speak in situations where speaking is expected, despite being able to speak in other situations. It is associated with anxiety and is not related to a lack of knowledge or comfort with the spoken language.

These are just a few examples of the many forms anxiety can take. Each person's experience with an anxiety disorder will be different, and two people with the same disorder may not experience it in the same way. However, all these disorders share a common thread: they involve disproportionate fear or anxiety that impairs daily functioning. The good news is that these disorders are treatable, and there are many effective therapies and interventions available. The first step, however, is understanding the nature of these disorders, which sets the stage for targeted, effective treatment.

Chapter 3: The Science of Anxiety

Understanding anxiety involves delving into the intricate labyrinth of human biology and psychology. Anxiety disorders, like many other mental health conditions, don't have a single cause. They emerge from a complex interplay of genetic, biological, environmental, and psychological factors.

Biological Causes of Anxiety

1. **Neurotransmitters**: Neurotransmitters are chemical messengers in the brain that transmit signals between nerve cells. Imbalances in neurotransmitters, such as serotonin, dopamine, and norepinephrine, have been linked to anxiety disorders. For instance, lower serotonin levels are associated with increased anxiety. In contrast, higher levels of norepinephrine, particularly in certain parts of the brain, have also been correlated with anxiety.
2. **Autonomic Nervous System**: This part of the nervous system regulates the body's unconscious actions, like heart rate, digestion, respiratory rate, pupillary response, and more. It's divided into the sympathetic and parasympathetic nervous systems. The sympathetic nervous system drives the "fight-or-flight" response, releasing adrenaline and cortisol, increasing heart rate, and diverting blood flow to muscles. When this system is activated excessively or inappropriately, it can lead to feelings of anxiety.
3. **Genetics**: Anxiety disorders can run in families, suggesting a genetic component in their development. If

a person has a close relative with an anxiety disorder, they are at a higher risk of developing one themselves. However, having a family history of anxiety doesn't guarantee that a person will develop an anxiety disorder. It's the interplay of genes and environment that determines this.

Psychological Causes of Anxiety

1. **Negative Thought Patterns**: People with anxiety disorders often engage in cognitive distortions, or faulty ways of thinking. These might include catastrophizing (expecting the worst possible outcome), overgeneralizing (applying one negative experience to all similar experiences), or black-and-white thinking (seeing things as only good or bad, with no middle ground). These thought patterns can trigger or exacerbate feelings of anxiety.
2. **Past Traumas**: Experiences from our past, particularly traumatic ones, can have a significant impact on our present mental health. People who've experienced abuse, violence, or severe stress might be more prone to anxiety disorders. This is particularly evident in post-traumatic stress disorder (PTSD), where anxiety symptoms are directly linked to a past traumatic event.
3. **Learned Behavior**: Some theories suggest that anxiety could be a learned behavior.

We might learn to feel anxious in response to certain situations because of experiences early in life. For instance, if a child has a parent who shows high levels of anxiety, they might 'learn' to react the same way.

Understanding the science of anxiety allows us to comprehend why we feel the way we do when we're anxious. It also provides the foundation for the development of effective treatment strategies, which we will explore in the following chapters.

While the above are some of the main factors contributing to anxiety, it's important to note that there is still much we don't understand about the science of anxiety. Research is ongoing and constantly shedding new light on the complex biological and psychological processes that contribute to these disorders.

Brain Structures: Various parts of the brain, especially those involved in managing fear and stress, play a role in maintaining anxiety. The amygdala, an almond-shaped structure in the brain, is pivotal in processing emotions and determining reactions to potentially threatening stimuli. Overactivity in the amygdala is associated with heightened anxiety. The hippocampus, involved in forming memories, also plays a role, particularly in conditions like PTSD where traumatic memories contribute to anxiety.

Hormonal Imbalances: The endocrine system, which produces hormones, has also been linked to anxiety. Cortisol, often called the 'stress hormone', can create feelings of anxiety if produced in excess. This can happen during times of chronic stress.

Underlying Health Conditions: Sometimes, anxiety may be a symptom of an underlying health condition. Conditions such as heart disease, diabetes, thyroid problems, respiratory disorders, and drug misuse or withdrawal can cause or exacerbate anxiety symptoms.

Anxiety disorders are undoubtedly complex, with no single cause. They're the result of a combination of factors, including genetics, brain chemistry, personality, and life events. How these elements interplay and how individuals respond to them may differ greatly, leading to the wide array of anxiety disorders we see. Understanding these elements, their roles, and interactions are crucial in designing effective treatments and coping strategies for individuals dealing with anxiety.

Chapter 4: The Physical Symptoms of Anxiety

Anxiety doesn't just affect the mind; it has profound physical manifestations as well. These physical symptoms can be just as distressing as the mental and emotional aspects of anxiety. It's crucial to recognize these symptoms and understand how to manage them effectively.

Common Physical Symptoms of Anxiety

1. **Accelerated Heart Rate**: One of the first signs of the fight-or-flight response is a quickened heartbeat. This can often feel like palpitations or a racing heart.
2. **Sweating**: During moments of anxiety, you may notice increased perspiration. This is another part of the body's stress response, intended to help cool the body down during perceived danger.
3. **Trembling or Shaking**: Shaking or trembling can also be a common symptom of anxiety. This is due to adrenaline surges in the body.
4. **Shortness of Breath**: Some people with anxiety report feeling short of breath or tightness in their chest. This can be a result of faster breathing or even hyperventilation, which is common during a panic attack.
5. **Stomach Upset**: Anxiety can also impact the digestive system, leading to symptoms like nausea, stomach upset, or diarrhea.
6. **Muscle Tension**: People with anxiety often experience chronic muscle tension. This can lead to headaches, neck tension, and other aches and pains throughout the body.

7. **Fatigue**: Over time, the constant state of worry and tension can leave individuals feeling fatigued or constantly tired.

8. **Insomnia**: Difficulty falling or staying asleep is common among individuals with anxiety disorders.

Managing Physical Symptoms of Anxiety

1. **Deep Breathing Techniques**: Deep, controlled breathing can be incredibly beneficial in managing symptoms like accelerated heart rate and shortness of breath. Try to breathe in for a count of four, hold your breath for a count of seven, and exhale for a count of eight. Repeat this cycle until your breathing and heart rate slow down.

Deep breathing techniques are simple yet powerful tools in managing anxiety. When we're anxious, we tend to take shallow, quick breaths (known as chest breathing or thoracic breathing), which can increase feelings of fear and anxiety. On the contrary, deep, slow breathing (or diaphragmatic breathing) can help calm the mind and body, regulate the heart rate, and stabilize blood pressure. Here are a few examples:

- **Box Breathing (or Square Breathing)**: This technique involves inhaling, holding the breath, exhaling, and holding the breath again, each for the same count (usually 4 seconds).

Practice: Close your eyes and take a deep breath, then exhale completely. Now, inhale slowly through your nose to a count of four, hold your breath for another count of four, then exhale through your mouth for a count of four. Lastly, hold your breath for a count of four again. Repeat this cycle several times.

- **4-7-8 Breathing**: This is a method developed by Dr. Andrew Weil, inspired by the ancient yogic technique called 'pranayama'.

  Practice: Begin by exhaling fully through your mouth. Then, close your mouth and inhale quietly through your nose to a count of four. Hold your breath for a count of seven. Finally, exhale completely through your mouth to a count of eight. This completes one breath. Now inhale again, and repeat the cycle three more times for a total of four breaths.

- **Belly Breathing (or Diaphragmatic Breathing)**: This technique emphasizes full breaths that come directly from the diaphragm, engaging the stomach and not just the chest.

Practice: Sit or lie down in a comfortable position. Place one hand on your chest and the other on your belly. Take a slow, deep breath in through your nose, allowing your belly to push against your hand. You should feel the hand on your belly rise more than the one on your chest. Exhale through your mouth, again noticing the hand on your belly falling more than the one on your chest. Try to breathe deeply and slowly, aiming for about six to ten breaths per minute. Practice for a few minutes each day.

Remember, the goal of these exercises is not just to perform them during moments of anxiety but to incorporate them into your daily routine. Over time, they can help reduce overall levels of stress and anxiety, improve focus and concentration, and promote a general sense of wellbeing.

2. **Progressive Muscle Relaxation (PMR)**: This technique involves tensing and then releasing different muscle groups to promote relaxation. PMR can be particularly effective for managing muscle tension and shaking.

Progressive Muscle Relaxation (PMR)

Progressive Muscle Relaxation (PMR) is a relaxation technique that involves systematically tensing and then releasing different muscle groups in your body. The goal is to induce a state of calm and promote physical relaxation, which can help manage symptoms of anxiety.

Here's a step-by-step guide on how to practice PMR:

- **Step 1**: Find a comfortable position. You can sit or lie down, whatever is more comfortable for you. Make sure you're in a quiet place where you won't be disturbed.
- **Step 2**: Start with your feet. Focus your mind on your right foot. Slowly tense the muscles as tightly as you can, hold for a count of 10, and then release. Notice the sensation of release and how different it feels from the tension.
- **Step 3**: Move up to your right calf. Repeat the process of tensing the muscle, holding, and then releasing.
- **Step 4**: Continue this process as you move up your body - your thigh, hip, stomach, chest, hand, arm, shoulders, neck, and finally, your face. Make sure to do both sides of your body.
- **Step 5**: Once you've tensed and relaxed each muscle group, spend a few minutes relaxing and breathing deeply and slowly. Notice how your body feels. Is it different from when you started?

Here's an example of how to tense and release muscles in the hand: Make a tight fist and hold it for a count of 10, focusing on the tension and tightness. Then, release your hand, spreading out your fingers and noticing the sensation of release and relaxation. Compare this feeling to the tension you felt just moments ago.

Remember, practice is key when it comes to relaxation techniques. The more you practice, the more naturally it will come to you, and the better you'll get at inducing relaxation in your body when you're feeling anxious. Always make sure to practice these techniques in a safe and comfortable environment, and if any exercise causes pain or discomfort, stop immediately and consider seeking advice from a healthcare provider.

3. **Regular Exercise**: Regular physical activity has been shown to reduce anxiety symptoms. It helps regulate the body's fight-or-flight response and promotes feelings of well-being.

Regular physical activity is beneficial for both physical and mental health. It can help reduce symptoms of anxiety by boosting mood, acting as a natural anti-anxiety treatment. Exercise helps increase the production of endorphins, the body's natural mood elevators, and reduce levels of the body's stress hormones, such as adrenaline and cortisol. Here are some examples of how to include regular exercise in your routine:

- **Walk or Jog**: Something as simple as a brisk walk or a light jog can be beneficial, especially if done regularly. Aim to walk or jog for at least 30 minutes a day. If 30 minutes at once seems too much, you can break it down into two or three shorter periods.

- **Yoga**: Yoga combines physical postures, breathing exercises, and meditation, making it an excellent exercise for reducing anxiety. Various styles suit different fitness levels and personal preferences, from gentle styles like Hatha yoga to more physically demanding styles like Vinyasa or Ashtanga.
- **Resistance Training**: This includes activities like lifting weights or bodyweight exercises. Resistance training can help reduce anxiety and improve mood.
- **Cycling**: Whether on a stationary bike or cycling outdoors, this can be a great way to reduce anxiety. It's also excellent for cardiovascular health.
- **Dance**: Dancing can be a fun way to exercise and can also act as a creative outlet, helping to further reduce anxiety.
- **Swimming**: Swimming is a low-impact exercise that is easy on the joints, and the water can have a calming effect.
- **Tai Chi or Qi Gong**: These are forms of gentle Chinese martial arts that involve flowing movements and deep breathing. They can help reduce anxiety and improve mood.

Remember, the goal is to find an activity you enjoy, so you'll be more likely to stick with it. Start slow and gradually increase the intensity and duration of your workouts over time. Before starting any new exercise regimen, it's always a good idea to consult with a healthcare provider, especially if you have any health concerns or medical conditions.

4. **Good Sleep Hygiene**: Maintaining regular sleep patterns and ensuring a calm, restful sleep environment can help manage anxiety-related insomnia.

Good sleep hygiene refers to habits that can help you have a good night's sleep. Regular, quality sleep can have a profound impact on overall health, and poor sleep can exacerbate symptoms of anxiety. Here are some examples of how to maintain good sleep hygiene:

- **Create a Sleep-Friendly Environment**: Make your bedroom a calm, quiet, and comfortable space. This might mean using blackout curtains, earplugs, or a white noise machine. The temperature should be cool, generally between 60-67 degrees Fahrenheit (15-19 degrees Celsius).
- **Establish a Regular Sleep Schedule**: Try to go to bed and wake up at the same time every day, even on weekends. This can help regulate your body's internal clock and promote better sleep.
- **Develop a Pre-Sleep Routine**: Engage in calming activities before bed such as reading, taking a warm bath, listening to soft music, or doing some gentle stretches. This can signal your body that it's time to wind down and go to sleep.

- **Limit Naps**: While napping isn't inherently bad, long or irregular naps can disrupt your sleep. If you need to nap, try to limit it to 20-30 minutes and make it during the early afternoon.
- **Mind Your Diet**: Avoid large meals, caffeine, and alcohol close to bedtime. These can disrupt your sleep cycle.
- **Turn Off Electronic Devices**: The light emitted by phones, tablets, computers, and TVs can interfere with the production of the sleep-inducing hormone melatonin. Try to turn off these devices at least an hour before bed.
- **Physical Activity**: Regular physical activity can help you fall asleep faster and enjoy deeper sleep. However, don't exercise too close to bedtime, as it might interfere with your sleep.
- **Manage Worries**: Anxiety and stress can interfere with sleep. Try to resolve your worries or concerns before bedtime. Techniques such as meditation or deep breathing can help you relax and manage any anxiety you might be feeling.

Remember, everyone's sleep needs and routines are different. What's most important is that you find and stick to a sleep routine that works for you. If you've tried these strategies and still have trouble sleeping, it might be time to consult a healthcare provider.

5. **Healthy Eating**: Maintaining a healthy diet and avoiding stimulants like caffeine and alcohol can also help regulate physical symptoms of anxiety.

A healthy diet can significantly impact mental health, including anxiety levels. Nutrient-rich foods can provide the necessary vitamins, minerals, and antioxidants your brain needs to function correctly and manage stress. Here are some strategies for incorporating healthy eating habits into your routine:

- **Eat a Balanced Diet**: Include a variety of foods from all the food groups - fruits, vegetables, whole grains, dairy, and protein. A diverse diet ensures your body gets a range of nutrients it needs to function optimally.
- **Limit Processed Foods**: Processed foods often contain high levels of sugar, unhealthy fats, and sodium, all of which can exacerbate anxiety symptoms. Try to limit your intake of these foods.
- **Stay Hydrated**: Dehydration can cause mood changes. Make sure to drink enough water each day. The amount can vary depending on various factors, but a general rule of thumb is to aim for eight 8-ounce glasses of water a day.
- **Eat Regular Meals**: Skipping meals can lead to drops in blood sugar, which can make you feel jittery and exacerbate feelings of anxiety. Try to eat regular, balanced meals throughout the day.

- **Limit Caffeine and Alcohol**: Both caffeine and alcohol can cause or worsen anxiety and can also interfere with sleep. Try to limit your consumption of both.
- **Omega-3 Fatty Acids**: Foods rich in omega-3 fatty acids, like salmon, sardines, chia seeds, flaxseeds, and walnuts, are good for brain health and may help reduce symptoms of anxiety.
- **Complex Carbohydrates**: Foods such as whole grains, brown rice, oatmeal, and sweet potatoes are rich in complex carbohydrates. These can increase the level of serotonin, a hormone that helps regulate mood, promoting feelings of relaxation and calm.
- **Lean Protein**: Foods like lean meat, poultry, fish, eggs, nuts, and legumes can help keep your blood sugar stable and prevent mood swings.
- **Probiotics and Fermented Foods**: Emerging research suggests that the gut-brain axis, the bidirectional communication link between the gut and the brain, plays a critical role in mental health. Foods like yogurt, sauerkraut, kefir, and kimchi, which are high in probiotics, can contribute to a healthy gut and potentially reduce anxiety.

Remember, everyone's nutritional needs are unique. Always consider seeking the advice of a registered dietitian or a healthcare professional for personalized dietary advice.

6. **Mindfulness and Meditation**: Practices such as yoga, mindfulness, and meditation can help you stay centered and grounded, reducing the intensity of physical anxiety symptoms over time.

Mindfulness and meditation are powerful tools for managing anxiety. They involve focusing your attention and eliminating the stream of thoughts that may be crowding your mind and causing stress. Here are some ways you can practice mindfulness and meditation:

- **Body Scan Meditation**: This technique involves paying attention to different parts of your body, from your toes to the crown of your head. Start by focusing on your toes and gradually move up your body, being aware of any tension, discomfort, or relaxation in each part.
- **Breathing Meditation**: Sit comfortably and close your eyes. Focus your attention on your breath, noticing how it feels as it enters and leaves your body. If your mind starts to wander, gently bring your focus back to your breathing.
- **Mindful Eating**: Instead of eating mindlessly in front of the TV or while working, take time to focus on your meal. Pay attention to the colors, smells, flavors, and textures of your food. Chew slowly and savor each bite.
- **Walking Meditation**: This involves focusing on the physical sensations of walking – the feeling of your feet touching the ground, the rhythm of your breath while moving, the wind against your face.

- **Loving-Kindness Meditation**: In this practice, you focus on developing feelings of compassion and love towards yourself and others. You silently repeat phrases like "May I be happy, may I be safe, may I be healthy, may I live with ease," and then extend these wishes to others.

- **Mindful Observation**: Choose an object in your environment and focus on it for a minute or two. It could be a flower, a painting, or anything else. Observe it as if you're seeing it for the first time. This practice can help you become more present and attentive.

- **Daily Mindfulness**: Incorporate mindfulness into your everyday life. This could be while brushing your teeth, taking a shower, or commuting. Be fully present in the moment, aware of your senses, emotions, and surroundings without judgment.

Remember, as with any skill, mindfulness and meditation require practice. Start with short sessions and gradually increase the duration as you get more comfortable with the practice. Even a few minutes of mindfulness and meditation each day can make a significant difference in reducing anxiety.

Recognizing and managing the physical symptoms of anxiety is a critical part of dealing with this disorder. However, it's also important to remember that these strategies are most effective when combined with broader treatment approaches, including therapy and medication, if recommended by a healthcare professional.

Chapter 5. Anxiety and Co-occurring Disorders

Anxiety rarely exists in isolation; it often co-occurs with other mental health disorders, creating a complex landscape that requires comprehensive understanding and treatment. This chapter delves into the common co-occurring disorders associated with anxiety, namely depression and post-traumatic stress disorder (PTSD), and discusses their treatment modalities.

Anxiety and Depression

The overlap between anxiety and depression is significant. Many people diagnosed with an anxiety disorder also have depression and vice versa. Both conditions share certain symptoms, such as irritability, problems with sleep and concentration, and a feeling of being on edge.

While these conditions have distinctive diagnostic criteria, they share a commonality in their treatment approaches. Both anxiety and depression are treated with a combination of psychotherapy (cognitive-behavioral therapy, or CBT, being particularly effective) and medication, usually selective serotonin reuptake inhibitors (SSRIs) or serotonin and norepinephrine reuptake inhibitors (SNRIs).

Lifestyle changes like regular exercise, a healthy diet, adequate sleep, reducing caffeine and alcohol intake, and mindfulness and relaxation techniques can also help manage both conditions. For individuals with both anxiety and depression, a tailored treatment plan addressing both disorders simultaneously is typically the most effective approach.

Anxiety and Post-Traumatic Stress Disorder (PTSD)

PTSD is a condition that can occur following the experience or witnessing of life-threatening events such as military combat, natural disasters, terrorist incidents, serious accidents, or physical or sexual assault. Individuals with PTSD often experience intense, disturbing thoughts and feelings related to their experience that last long after the traumatic event has ended.

Like anxiety, PTSD disrupts life and causes considerable distress. Anxiety disorders, particularly panic disorder and generalized anxiety disorder, frequently co-occur with PTSD, further complicating the symptom picture.

Treatment for PTSD often involves a combination of psychotherapy and medication. Cognitive Processing Therapy (CPT) and Prolonged Exposure (PE) therapy are specific types of CBT used to treat PTSD. Eye Movement Desensitization and Reprocessing (EMDR) is another form of therapy used in PTSD treatment. Medications, including SSRIs and SNRIs, are also used to alleviate the symptoms of PTSD and any co-occurring anxiety disorder.

Recognizing the interconnected nature of these disorders is crucial. Comprehensive treatment plans that address all co-occurring conditions tend to offer the best outcomes, helping individuals regain control and start their journey towards healing and recovery.

Chapter 6. Anxiety Treatments: Therapy

Therapy forms a cornerstone of anxiety treatment. Various therapeutic approaches can help individuals cope with and manage their anxiety, addressing both the physiological and psychological aspects of the disorder. This chapter will delve into two types of therapy particularly effective in treating anxiety - Cognitive Behavioral Therapy (CBT) and Acceptance and Commitment Therapy (ACT).

Cognitive Behavioral Therapy (CBT)

CBT is a widely recognized and effective treatment for anxiety. It's based on the idea that our thoughts (cognition) and actions (behavior) interact and influence each other, contributing to our mental health and overall well-being.

In CBT, therapists work with individuals to identify, understand, and change negative thought patterns that lead to anxiety symptoms. By learning to recognize and alter these thought patterns, individuals can better manage their response to anxiety-provoking situations.

Consider the case of Sarah, a patient who sought CBT for her generalized anxiety disorder. Through therapy, she learned to identify her anxiety-provoking thoughts (such as assuming she would fail in everything she does) and replace them with more positive, realistic affirmations. She reported that CBT helped reduce her anxiety symptoms and improved her overall outlook on life.

Acceptance and Commitment Therapy (ACT)

ACT is another therapeutic approach used to treat anxiety. The focus of ACT is to help individuals accept their thoughts and feelings rather than trying to change or eliminate them. It emphasizes mindfulness, acceptance, and values-based living.

In ACT, individuals learn to observe their anxious thoughts and feelings without judgement, to recognize them as transient rather than defining aspects of themselves. The goal is to reduce the impact and influence of these thoughts and feelings, allowing individuals to act in ways aligned with their personal values, even in the presence of anxiety.

James, an individual who undertook ACT for his panic disorder, shares his experience. He learned to accept his panic attacks as something he experiences, not something that defines him. He practiced mindfulness exercises to stay grounded during episodes and focused on living according to his values despite the presence of anxiety. James found that while his panic attacks didn't completely disappear, their impact on his life decreased significantly, and he felt more in control.

Therapy provides a safe and supportive environment to explore and address anxiety. With the guidance of a skilled therapist, individuals can gain valuable insights and tools to manage their anxiety effectively. The journey of therapy differs for everyone, but the testimonies of many echo the transformative impact it can have on their lives.

Expanding the scope of treatment options for anxiety, there exist alternative therapies that some people find beneficial, particularly when used in conjunction with traditional therapies. These include herbal remedies, nutritional supplements, and other natural treatments that can help alleviate symptoms of anxiety. However, it's essential to note that while these methods can provide relief, they do not substitute professional medical advice and treatment.

Herbal Remedies and Nutritional Supplements

Certain herbs and nutritional supplements have been studied for their potential to reduce anxiety symptoms. For instance, chamomile is often used in the form of a tea and has been found to have mild sedative effects, potentially reducing anxiety symptoms.

Another example is Kava, a plant native to the South Pacific, often used in traditional medicine to alleviate anxiety. Clinical studies have shown that kava can be effective in reducing anxiety symptoms, although it should be used under medical supervision due to potential liver toxicity.

Valerian root, often used as a sleep aid, may also help reduce anxiety. It can be consumed as a tea, tincture, or in capsule form.

Omega-3 fatty acids, found in fish oil, have been studied for their role in brain health and function. Some research suggests they may help reduce anxiety, though more studies are needed to confirm these findings.

Aromatherapy

Aromatherapy uses aromatic essential oils to promote health and well-being. Certain scents like lavender, chamomile, and sandalwood are often used for their calming and soothing effects.

Acupuncture

Acupuncture is a practice in traditional Chinese medicine involving the insertion of thin needles into specific points on the body. Some studies suggest that acupuncture may help reduce symptoms of anxiety.

Yoga and Tai Chi

These practices combine physical postures, breathing exercises, and meditation to promote physical and mental well-being. Both yoga and Tai Chi have been found to reduce anxiety and stress, improve mood, and enhance overall quality of life.

Remember, while these therapies can provide relief, they should not replace traditional treatment for anxiety disorders. Always consult with a healthcare provider before starting any new treatment or supplement, as they can interact with other medications and treatments, and they may not be appropriate for everyone.

Chapter 7. Anxiety Treatments: Medication (RX)

Medication, often in combination with psychotherapy, is a crucial part of anxiety treatment. Several types of medication can help alleviate the symptoms of anxiety, allowing individuals to lead more functional and fulfilling lives. This chapter will focus on three primary types of medication used to treat anxiety - Benzodiazepines, Selective Serotonin Reuptake Inhibitors (SSRIs), and Serotonin and Norepinephrine Reuptake Inhibitors (SNRIs).

Benzodiazepines

Benzodiazepines, such as Xanax (alprazolam), Ativan (lorazepam), and Valium (diazepam), are often used for short-term relief of acute symptoms, like a panic attack. They work quickly, typically bringing relief within 30 minutes to an hour. Benzodiazepines act on the central nervous system, producing a sedative effect that can help reduce anxiety.

However, because of their potential for addiction and withdrawal, they are typically not the first choice for long-term management of chronic anxiety. Common side effects include drowsiness, dizziness, nausea, and potential memory impairment.

Selective Serotonin Reuptake Inhibitors (SSRIs)

SSRIs are a type of antidepressant that can also help treat anxiety disorders. They increase the level of serotonin, a neurotransmitter that helps regulate mood, in the brain. Commonly prescribed SSRIs include Prozac (fluoxetine), Zoloft (sertraline), and Lexapro (escitalopram).

SSRIs typically take a few weeks to start working, making them more suitable for chronic anxiety symptoms rather than acute panic attacks. Side effects can include nausea, dry mouth, muscle weakness, diarrhea, and sexual dysfunction.

Serotonin and Norepinephrine Reuptake Inhibitors (SNRIs)

Like SSRIs, SNRIs are a type of antidepressant that can be used to treat anxiety. They increase levels of serotonin and norepinephrine, another neurotransmitter related to mood, in the brain. Examples include Effexor (venlafaxine) and Cymbalta (duloxetine).

SNRIs also take a few weeks to start showing effects. Potential side effects are similar to those of SSRIs.

Choosing the right medication for anxiety depends on a variety of factors, including the type of anxiety disorder, the individual's specific symptoms, the presence of any co-occurring psychiatric and medical conditions, the potential side effects, and interactions with other medications.

It's important to discuss all these factors with a healthcare provider who can guide the process and monitor for any adverse effects. While medications can provide significant relief from anxiety, they are typically most effective when used in combination with therapy and healthy lifestyle changes.

Chapter 8. The Role of Music in Managing Anxiety

The therapeutic use of music has been recognized throughout history and across cultures. Music can evoke a wide range of emotions and can be an effective tool in managing anxiety. This chapter delves into the role of music in anxiety management and explores ways to harness its power for therapeutic benefits.

The Power of Music

Music, often referred to as a universal language, has a profound ability to touch our hearts, stir our emotions, and alter our mood. Its capacity to connect with the deepest layers of the human psyche has been recognized since antiquity, and modern science has added to this understanding by uncovering the neural mechanisms underlying music's impact.

When we listen to music, it engages widespread brain regions involved in cognition, emotion, and motor control. Music, with its beat, melody, and lyrics, can stimulate our minds, evoke a wide range of emotions, and even provoke physical responses, such as foot-tapping or dancing.

Fast-paced music, with a high tempo or a strong beat, can have an invigorating effect. It can stimulate the release of adrenaline, increase heart rate and blood pressure, and sharpen the mental state. This can generate feelings of excitement and anticipation, and such music can be used when we need a boost of energy or motivation. However, if one is already in a state of anxiety, fast-paced music may heighten those feelings and might be best avoided.

In contrast, slow-paced music, especially with a rhythm of about 60 beats per minute, can slow the heart rate, reduce blood pressure, and lower stress hormones. It can induce a state of tranquility, helping to slow down thought processes and relax tense muscles. Genres like classical music, ambient soundscapes, or certain kinds of world music can often offer such slower rhythms. This calming effect of music can be particularly useful in anxiety management.

Music can also serve as a means of emotional expression. For individuals dealing with anxiety, it may sometimes be challenging to articulate feelings verbally. In such cases, music - either listening to resonant pieces or creating it - can provide an alternative means of expressing and processing emotions.

Moreover, music can serve as a useful distraction from anxious thoughts. The process of engaging with music—following along with the lyrics, getting absorbed in the melody, or focusing on the instruments—can draw attention away from worry and negative thought cycles. It provides a focal point, a center of attention that is separate from one's anxiety.

It's important to note that music is a highly personal experience, and different people may respond differently to the same piece of music. Thus, the use of music in managing anxiety should be personalized, catering to one's unique musical preferences and emotional needs.

From resonance with our emotions to impact on our physiology, music harnesses a variety of channels to exert its powerful effects. Its role as a non-pharmaceutical, accessible tool in managing anxiety continues to be relevant, serving as a testament to the extraordinary power of music.

Music Therapy

Music therapy, a recognized therapeutic modality, harnesses the innate power of music to promote healing and enhance quality of life. It involves the use of musical experiences such as listening, singing, or playing an instrument to accomplish individualized therapeutic goals within a professional relationship.

A key strength of music therapy lies in its versatility. It can be used to address a broad range of physical, emotional, cognitive, and social needs. In the context of anxiety, music therapy can provide a non-threatening environment where individuals can express their feelings, explore their concerns, and develop coping strategies.

Music therapy for anxiety often begins with a comprehensive assessment to understand the person's needs, musical preferences, and level of comfort with various forms of musical engagement. This helps the therapist tailor a personalized therapeutic plan that might include active music making, receptive music listening, improvisation, songwriting, or even guided imagery with music.

Active Music Making

This includes playing an instrument, singing, or engaging in rhythm-based activities. For individuals dealing with anxiety, actively creating music can provide a tangible sense of control and accomplishment. It also allows for the expression of feelings that might be difficult to articulate in words.

Receptive Music Listening

Receptive music listening involves attentively listening to live or recorded music selected by the therapist. This method can be used to facilitate relaxation, distract from anxious thoughts, and stimulate emotional release.

Improvisation

Improvisation, or creating music on the spot, provides an avenue for spontaneous expression. It enables individuals to externalize their internal emotional state, and in the process, gain new insights into their feelings and reactions.

Songwriting

Songwriting in music therapy provides an opportunity for individuals to put their thoughts, feelings, and experiences into words and music. This process can give voice to experiences of anxiety, help in reframing negative thought patterns, and foster a sense of agency and empowerment.

Guided Imagery and Music

In this method, individuals listen to carefully chosen pieces of music while the therapist guides them in visualizing images, scenes, or narratives. This can help individuals explore their subconscious, gain new perspectives, and find inner resources for managing anxiety.

An important aspect of music therapy is the therapeutic relationship that develops between the therapist and the individual. The therapist provides a safe, accepting, and supportive environment that facilitates self-exploration and growth.

While music therapy can be a potent tool for managing anxiety, it's essential to remember that it is one component of a comprehensive anxiety management plan. It should be used in conjunction with other strategies, such as cognitive-behavioral therapy, medication, and lifestyle changes, for optimal benefits.

Creating a Personalized Playlist

Creating a personalized playlist can be a simple and effective way to manage anxiety. It can be helpful to have different playlists for different needs - a calming playlist for when anxiety is high, an uplifting playlist for when mood needs a boost, and a comforting playlist for when you need solace.

Active vs. Passive Listening

There are two main ways to use music for anxiety management - active and passive listening. Active listening involves engaging fully with the music, such as by playing an instrument or using music as a backdrop for meditation. Passive listening can also be beneficial and involves having music play in the background during other activities. Both methods can be effective and can be chosen based on personal preference and situation.

Singing and Playing Instruments

Engaging in music-making can also be therapeutic. Singing, in particular, can be a powerful tool for releasing emotions and reducing anxiety. Playing an instrument can have similar benefits and can provide a focus point, helping to distract from anxious thoughts.

Incorporating music into your anxiety management strategies can provide an additional tool in your toolbox. However, it's essential to remember that while music can be a powerful adjunctive therapy, it does not replace the need for professional help in cases of severe or chronic anxiety disorders. Always consult with a healthcare provider or a certified music therapist to discuss how best to incorporate music into your anxiety management plan.

Chapter 9. Embracing Mindfulness: A Powerful Ally Against Anxiety

Mindfulness, a state of active, open attention to the present moment, has emerged as a potent ally in managing anxiety. Rooted in ancient contemplative practices and now validated by contemporary science, mindfulness offers a path to quiet the mind, live more fully in the present, and reduce the grip of anxiety. This chapter explores the theory and practice of mindfulness for anxiety management and provides practical tips for incorporating it into daily life.

Understanding Mindfulness

At the heart of mindfulness is a simple yet profound concept: cultivating a deliberate, non-judgmental awareness of the present moment. This heightened state of presence and consciousness allows us to tune into our current experiences - our thoughts, feelings, and sensations - without the filters of bias or judgment.

1. **Awareness:** Mindfulness requires us to be keenly aware of what we're sensing and feeling at every moment, without interpretation or judgment. This involves an intimate engagement with the world around us and our inner landscapes. It's about noticing the sensation of the wind against our skin, the taste of food, the sound of birds, or the rumbling thoughts in our minds.
2. **Non-Judgment:** Practicing mindfulness means observing these experiences without labeling them as

good or bad, right or wrong, fair or unfair. Instead, we learn to view our thoughts and feelings as passing phenomena. This non-judgmental stance allows us to open up to our experiences rather than resisting or trying to control them.

3. **Present Moment Focus:** Mindfulness is rooted in the present. Instead of dwelling on the past or anticipating the future, we anchor our attention in the now. By being fully engaged in the present moment, we can encounter our everyday experiences as they truly are, moment by moment.

In the context of anxiety, mindfulness's emphasis on present-moment awareness can be particularly beneficial. Often, anxiety is driven by worries about the future or ruminations on the past. By training our attention on the present, we learn to disengage from these anxiety-provoking thought patterns.

When we practice mindfulness, we learn to observe our anxious thoughts and feelings as they arise, but critically, without getting entangled in them. We begin to see that these are just thoughts, transient and ephemeral, and not objective truths. With time, this ability to observe rather than react to our anxious thoughts can reduce their impact and influence over us.

For example, instead of thinking "I'm feeling anxious because I'll do terrible in my presentation," mindfulness encourages a different perspective: "I'm noticing the thought that I'll do terrible in my presentation and the accompanying feeling of anxiety."

Such a shift may seem small, but it can make a significant difference in managing anxiety. By adopting this observing stance, we create a mental space between ourselves and our thoughts, reducing their immediacy and intensity. This provides us with the opportunity to respond to our anxiety in more adaptive and less distressing ways.

The Science Behind Mindfulness and Anxiety

The effectiveness of mindfulness in reducing symptoms of anxiety is not just anecdotal. It's supported by a substantial body of scientific research, indicating a clear neurological basis for its benefits. By promoting a shift in the brain's focus of attention, mindfulness can disrupt the often self-perpetuating cycle of anxious rumination and worry.

1. **Mindfulness and the Brain:** Neuroimaging studies have shown that mindfulness practices can lead to significant changes in brain structures associated with perception, body awareness, pain tolerance, emotion regulation, introspection, complex thinking, and sense of self. For instance, consistent mindfulness practice can increase the density of the prefrontal cortex, an area associated with higher order brain functions such as awareness, concentration, and decision-making.

2. **Shifting Attentional Focus:** Mindfulness facilitates a shift in the brain's attentional focus away from its "default mode network" (DMN), which is active when

our minds wander, often towards ruminative, self-referential thoughts. When the DMN is overactive, it can lead to patterns of ruminative, negative thinking that contribute to anxiety. By training our minds to focus on the present moment, mindfulness helps quiet this default network, reducing rumination and worry.

3. **Reducing Amygdala Reactivity:** The amygdala, often referred to as the brain's "fear center", plays a crucial role in how we respond to threats and anxiety-provoking situations. Studies have shown that mindfulness can reduce amygdala reactivity and increase connectivity between the amygdala and prefrontal cortex. This helps improve our ability to regulate emotional responses, reducing the intensity and frequency of anxiety symptoms.

4. **Enhancing Emotional Regulation:** Mindfulness promotes better emotional regulation by helping us disengage from emotionally upsetting pictures and enabling us to focus better on a cognitive task. As we become more aware of our emotional states, we gain greater agency over our reactions and responses to stressful events.

5. **Improving Stress Response:** Mindfulness can affect our physiological response to stress, including a reduction in heart rate, blood pressure, and cortisol levels. This can help create a sense of calm and relaxation, reducing the physical symptoms often associated with anxiety.

In summary, the practice of mindfulness has been shown to bring about changes in brain structure and function that are beneficial for reducing anxiety symptoms. It does so by shifting our attentional focus, improving emotional regulation, reducing reactivity to perceived threats, and improving our physiological stress response. By disrupting the cycle of negative thoughts and physiological responses that fuel anxiety, mindfulness creates a pathway towards greater mental calm and resilience.

Practicing Mindfulness Meditation

Mindfulness meditation is a structured approach to cultivating mindfulness, a state of focused attention on the present moment. This practice often involves dedicating a set time each day to enter a state of mindful awareness, concentrating on various aspects of your sensory experience.

1. **Breath Awareness:** This form of mindfulness meditation directs your focus to the rhythm of your breath as it enters and leaves your body. By concentrating solely on your breathing, you gradually learn to tune out distractions and calm the mind. This can not only reduce symptoms of anxiety, but also foster a sense of tranquility and relaxation.
2. **Body Scan Meditation:** In this practice, attention is methodically directed to different parts of the body, from your toes to the top of your head. As you mentally scan each part of your body, you become aware of

physical sensations, including pain, tension, warmth, or relaxation. This form of mindfulness meditation can heighten body awareness and promote a deeper mind-body connection, crucial in managing anxiety.

3. **Emotion-Focused Meditation:** Some mindfulness meditations involve focusing on specific emotions. Here, instead of trying to avoid or change your feelings, you learn to observe them without judgment. This can be particularly beneficial in managing anxiety, as it allows you to face your fears and anxieties in a controlled, safe environment.

4. **Mindfulness of Thoughts:** This practice involves observing your thoughts as they arise and fade, without becoming attached to them. By visualizing thoughts as clouds passing in the sky or leaves floating on a stream, you can learn to let go of anxiety-provoking thoughts, reducing their power over you.

5. **Loving-Kindness Meditation:** Also known as Metta meditation, this form of mindfulness practice involves directing positive feelings of love and compassion towards yourself and others. This practice can reduce negative self-judgment, a common feature of anxiety, and promote feelings of kindness and self-acceptance.

Scientific research has consistently shown that mindfulness meditation can have profound effects on mental health. Notably, it has been found to reduce symptoms of anxiety and increase feelings of calm and relaxation. These benefits are attributed to changes in brain function and structure, as well as improvements in emotional regulation and stress response. By incorporating mindfulness meditation into daily routines, individuals struggling with anxiety can cultivate greater emotional resilience and an enhanced sense of well-being.

Mindful Breathing

Breath-focused mindfulness, also referred to as mindfulness of breathing, is a fundamental practice in mindfulness meditation. It is an accessible starting point for those new to meditation and serves as a powerful tool for calming the mind and reducing anxiety. This practice is centered on the continual focus on the breath, its rhythm, and sensation.

1. **Observing the Breath:** Start by finding a comfortable position in a quiet space where you won't be disturbed. Begin to breathe naturally and turn your attention to your breath, noticing how it moves in and out of your body. Observe the rise and fall of your chest or the sensation of the breath as it enters and exits your nostrils.
2. **Staying with the Breath:** The aim is to keep your attention focused on the breath. Feel the cool air entering your body and the warm air leaving it. Notice the spaces between the breaths, the inhales and exhales. Try to engage fully with the process of breathing, noting the physical sensations and the quiet moments in between.

3. **Returning to the Breath:** It's natural for the mind to wander away from the breath and get caught up in different thoughts. When you notice that your mind has drifted, gently but firmly bring your focus back to your breath. The act of noticing the mind-wandering and choosing to return focus to the breath is at the core of mindfulness practice.

4. **Non-Judgmental Awareness:** Approach this exercise with a sense of patience and curiosity. If you find yourself getting frustrated with the wandering mind, remember that this is part of the practice and an opportunity for mindfulness. The goal is not to empty your mind of thoughts but to cultivate an awareness of the present moment.

5. **Regular Practice:** Like any skill, mindfulness improves with regular practice. Dedicate a specific time each day to this exercise, even if it's just for a few minutes. Over time, you may find that your mind wanders less and that you're able to maintain focus on your breath for longer periods.

This simple yet effective practice can have profound benefits for anxiety. By anchoring your focus on the breath, you can create a space of calm amidst the chaos of anxious thoughts. It provides a respite from the automatic reactions that often fuel anxiety, fostering a sense of peace and relaxation instead.

Body Scan

The body scan is a mindfulness practice that enhances your connection to your physical presence and can help alleviate symptoms of anxiety. It involves methodically shifting your focus through different parts of your body, starting from your toes and working your way up to the top of your head.

1. **Starting Position:** Begin by finding a quiet, comfortable place where you can lie down on your back without interruptions. Close your eyes and take a few deep breaths, allowing yourself to settle into the space.
2. **Focusing on the Feet:** Start your body scan at your feet. Notice any sensations you feel, such as warmth, coolness, heaviness, or perhaps nothing at all. Don't judge these sensations or try to change them, just note them and move on.
3. **Moving Upwards:** Gradually move your attention up through the body — your ankles, calves, knees, thighs, and so on. At each point, pause to notice any physical sensations, whether they're pain, tension, comfort, or numbness.
4. **Being Present with Sensations:** If you encounter areas of tension or discomfort, try not to shy away from them. Instead, acknowledge them and breathe into these areas. The goal isn't to change or eliminate these sensations but to notice them without judgement.
5. **Releasing Tension:** As you move through each part of your body, imagine each breath flowing to that body

part. As you breathe out, visualize tension leaving your body. This can enhance the relaxation effect of the body scan practice.

6. **Completing the Scan:** Continue to scan your body all the way up to the top of your head. When you're finished, take a moment to feel your body as a whole. Notice the sensations of your body making contact with the surface beneath you.

7. **Returning to the Day:** When you're ready, gently wiggle your fingers and toes, slowly open your eyes, and come back to the room. Try to carry this sense of body awareness into the rest of your day.

The body scan can be a powerful tool for managing anxiety. By tuning into the body and its sensations, you can divert your attention away from anxious thoughts. Furthermore, the body scan can foster a greater mind-body connection, an essential aspect of anxiety management and overall wellness. It is recommended to perform this practice regularly to fully experience its benefits.

Mindful Eating

Mindful eating is a form of mindfulness practice that brings your full attention to the process of eating. It's about savoring each bite and appreciating the food in front of you, thereby transforming a routine act into a powerful mindfulness practice. It can also enhance your relationship with food and help manage anxiety symptoms.

1. **Setting the Scene:** Start by reducing distractions. This could mean turning off the TV, putting away your phone, or finding a quiet place to eat. This prepares an environment conducive to mindful eating.
2. **Observing Your Food:** Before you begin eating, take a moment to look at your food. Notice the colors, textures, and aroma. Consider where it came from and the effort taken to prepare it.
3. **Eating Slowly:** When you start eating, take smaller bites and chew slowly. Try to identify the different flavors and textures in your mouth. This not only improves digestion but also allows you to savor each bite.
4. **Paying Attention to Hunger and Fullness Cues:** Part of mindful eating is learning to listen to your body's signals for hunger and fullness. Try to eat when you're genuinely hungry and stop when you're comfortably full.
5. **Noticing Your Reaction:** Pay attention to how different foods make you feel, both physically and emotionally. Are there certain foods that make you feel

sluggish or energetic? Do some foods bring up certain memories or emotions?

6. **Appreciating Your Food:** Show gratitude for your meal. This could involve expressing thanks for the nourishment it provides, or for the people involved in its preparation and delivery.

Mindful eating can bring a sense of calm and satisfaction that can help reduce anxiety. It forces you to slow down and focus on the present moment, rather than being swept up in anxious thoughts. By fully engaging with the experience of eating, you can turn a simple daily act into a powerful tool for mindfulness and anxiety relief. Remember, like any other mindfulness practice, mindful eating takes time and patience to master. The key is consistent practice.

Incorporating Mindfulness into Daily Life

Informal mindfulness practice refers to infusing mindful awareness into our everyday activities. This could involve things as mundane as brushing your teeth, taking a shower, or walking. These moments, often performed on autopilot, offer tremendous opportunities for mindfulness practice. They serve as reminders that any moment can be a mindful moment.

1. **Mindful Toothbrushing:** Instead of letting your mind wander while brushing your teeth, pay attention to the experience. Feel the bristles against your teeth and gums,

taste the toothpaste, and listen to the sounds of brushing. This simple practice can set a mindful tone for the day.

2. **Mindful Showering:** When taking a shower, notice the sensation of water on your skin. Observe the temperature, the feeling of droplets trickling down, the scent of soap. Make the shower a moment of relaxation and presence, not just a routine task.

3. **Mindful Walking:** Whether it's walking to the store or taking a leisurely stroll, focus on the experience. Feel the ground beneath your feet, notice your surroundings, the sounds, smells, and sights.

4. **Mindful Eating:** As discussed earlier, turn your meals into a mindfulness session by focusing on each bite, savoring the taste and texture, and listening to your body's fullness cues.

5. **Mindful Breathing:** Take a few minutes every hour to focus on your breath. Pay attention to the rise and fall of your chest, the sensation of air entering and leaving your nostrils. This can serve as a quick mindfulness exercise amidst a busy day.

Remember, the goal of informal mindfulness practice isn't to reach a state of perpetual mindfulness, but rather to weave moments of mindfulness into your day. It's these small moments that collectively make a significant difference in managing anxiety.

Mindfulness, like any other skill, requires practice and patience. However, its potential benefits in managing anxiety and improving overall well-being make it a worthwhile endeavor. Mindfulness is not about achieving a specific state or feeling a certain way but about noticing what's happening in the present moment. In that noticing, we can find a sense of calm and peace amidst the chaos of life. Whether through formal meditation or everyday tasks, cultivating mindfulness can serve as a powerful tool in your anxiety management toolkit.

Chapter 10: Positive Affirmations: A Necessity for Anxious Individuals

Anxiety is a widespread mental health issue affecting millions of individuals globally. It can manifest as a chronic disorder or occasional bouts of overwhelming worry and fear. For people grappling with anxiety, their everyday lives can become a tumultuous landscape of unsettling thoughts and emotional upheavals. Amid this, the power of positive affirmations often emerges as a critical tool that can provide relief and instigate constructive shifts in mindset.

Positive affirmations are self-reinforcing statements that one makes to oneself, often characterized by optimism and acceptance. The science behind positive affirmations involves the neuroplasticity of the brain - the ability of the brain to modify its connections or rewire itself. By repeating positive affirmations, we can create new neural pathways that promote positive thought patterns and emotions, helping to mitigate anxiety.

One of the significant benefits of positive affirmations is their capacity to counter negative thoughts and self-talk, which are prevalent in individuals experiencing anxiety. These negative thought patterns can often create a cycle of worry that perpetuates the anxious feelings. However, by consciously choosing to replace these negative thoughts with positive affirmations, individuals can break this cycle, thus reducing their anxiety.

For instance, instead of falling prey to thoughts such as "I can't handle this" or "Everything is going wrong," one can use positive affirmations such as "I am capable of handling whatever comes my way" or "Every situation is manageable and temporary." These affirmations not only shift focus from negativity to positivity but also reinforce a sense of personal power and self-efficacy, which is often diminished in anxious individuals.

Moreover, positive affirmations can help build self-esteem and self-confidence, two crucial elements often compromised in those battling anxiety. Affirmations such as "I am worthy" and "I believe in my abilities" can help boost the perception of self-worth, thus providing a solid base for overcoming anxiety and fears.

The practice of positive affirmations also promotes mindfulness and presence, drawing attention away from past or future worries and grounding individuals in the here and now. This serves as an excellent coping mechanism to keep anxiety at bay, as it helps individuals recognize that they are not their anxiety, but rather observers of it.

While the utility of positive affirmations may seem simple, their transformative potential should not be underestimated. Regular practice of this technique can bring about profound changes in an individual's perception of self and life, offering a robust defense against the debilitating grips of anxiety.

In conclusion, positive affirmations, when practiced consistently and authentically, can be a crucial tool for anxious individuals. They can break the cycle of negative self-talk, boost self-esteem, promote mindfulness, and foster a greater sense of control over one's thoughts and emotions. As such, they form a critical component in the toolbox for managing and reducing anxiety, fostering a more optimistic and positive life experience.

Chapter 11 Removing Negative Influences and Toxic Individuals

The Psychological Toll of Sensationalized News

In the hyper-connected world we live in, news, especially sensationalized news, has a far-reaching and immediate impact. Sensationalized news refers to the style of reporting that emphasizes the unusual, shocking, or dramatic aspects of stories, often at the expense of providing balanced information.

The omnipresence of such sensationalized news can have severe psychological effects, leading to heightened anxiety, stress, and fear. It can make one feel constantly on edge, as if the world is perpetually in crisis. Sensationalized news can also distort one's perspective of reality, leading to an overestimation of danger or risk.

In individuals already prone to anxiety, exposure to sensationalized news can amplify feelings of dread and worry, creating a chronic state of unease. The overemphasis on fear, danger, and negativity can trigger the body's stress response, causing a range of physical symptoms such as increased heart rate, disturbed sleep patterns, and overall unease. It can lead to a vicious cycle, where the exposure to negative news induces anxiety, and this anxiety, in turn, heightens the sensitivity to such news, exacerbating the distress.

How Negative News Fuels Anxiety

The relationship between negative news and anxiety is rooted in our biological makeup. As humans, we have a negativity bias - a tendency to pay more attention to negative information as it has more potential to harm us. This bias served us well in ancient times when survival often hinged on being alert to threats. However, in today's world, it can lead to disproportionate anxiety and stress.

Negative news stories, which are more common than positive ones, feed into this bias. Every report about disasters, violence, or crisis reinforces our fears and worries. Over time, this constant exposure to negative news can alter our perception of the world, making it appear more dangerous than it actually is.

Moreover, the immediacy and intrusiveness of modern news, where distressing images and headlines can appear unbidden on our screens at any time, leave little room for psychological respite. For those with anxiety, this can create a sense of being trapped in a never-ending cycle of negativity and fear.

In conclusion, understanding the psychological impact of sensationalized and negative news is a crucial first step in managing its influence on our lives. It empowers us to make informed decisions about our news consumption, guarding our mental health, and maintaining a balanced perspective of the world.

Strategies to Manage News Exposure

Implementing Designated 'News Hours'

Designating specific 'news hours' can be a powerful strategy to manage the anxiety triggered by continuous news consumption. This involves setting aside particular times of the day when you allow yourself to catch up on the news, and consciously avoiding it at other times.

Firstly, it's vital to avoid starting your day with news, particularly negative news. Begin your morning with activities that relax and rejuvenate you, setting a positive tone for the rest of the day. Similarly, refrain from consuming news right before bed, as it could impact your sleep quality, especially if it's distressing.

A 'news hour' could be scheduled during the mid-day or early evening, times when you're better equipped to handle any negative information. Limit these 'news hours' to a reasonable duration, perhaps no more than half an hour to one hour, and ensure to counterbalance it with positive or neutral content.

This structured approach provides a sense of control over your news consumption, helping to reduce feelings of anxiety and overwhelm.

Selecting Reliable and Balanced News Sources

Not all news sources are created equal. While some provide reliable, balanced coverage, others tend to sensationalize or focus predominantly on negative stories. Thus, it's crucial to consciously select your news sources.

Opt for news outlets that are reputed for their factual accuracy, balanced reporting, and ethical journalism. These sources provide a more nuanced view of world events, preventing the skewing of perspective that can arise from sensationalized news.

Consider diversifying your news sources, including local, national, and international perspectives. This can help you gain a broader, more balanced understanding of the world, rather than a narrow, fear-based narrative.

Furthermore, explore platforms that focus on positive or solution-based news. These sources can serve as an antidote to the negativity often found in mainstream news, offering inspiring stories of resilience, innovation, and kindness.

By implementing designated 'news hours' and consciously selecting reliable, balanced news sources, you can manage your news exposure effectively. This not only helps keep anxiety at bay but also encourages a healthier, more informed engagement with the world around you.

The Traits of Toxic Individuals

Toxic individuals possess characteristics that can deplete your energy, undermine your self-esteem, and exacerbate anxiety. Understanding these traits can help in identifying such individuals and taking necessary measures to protect your mental well-being.

A common trait of toxic individuals is consistent negativity. They often have a pessimistic outlook on life, are prone to criticism, and may frequently engage in negative talk. This perpetual negativity can bring down your mood and breed an environment of anxiety and stress.

Another trait is a lack of empathy or disregard for your feelings. Toxic individuals often prioritize their needs and feelings over others, showing little concern for the emotional impact of their actions or words. They may belittle your feelings or experiences, leaving you feeling invalidated or disrespected.

Toxic individuals may also be manipulative, using tactics like guilt-tripping or gaslighting to influence your behavior or perception. They might play the victim or twist facts to serve their narrative, causing you to question your reality or judgment.

Lastly, toxic individuals often resist boundaries. They may demand your time and attention excessively or disregard your personal boundaries, leading to feelings of discomfort and anxiety.

Identifying Toxicity in Personal Relationships

Identifying toxicity in personal relationships involves recognizing the signs of toxic behavior and understanding how these interactions affect your mental and emotional state.

Start by observing how you feel after interactions with various people in your life. Do you feel drained, anxious, or belittled? Do you often feel the need to justify your actions or suppress your feelings in their presence? These could be signs that the individual is toxic.

Reflect on the nature of your interactions with them. Are they characterized by respect, reciprocity, and understanding, or are they dominated by criticism, manipulation, and negativity? A consistent pattern of the latter could indicate a toxic relationship.

Finally, listen to your intuition. Often, your gut feelings can guide you towards recognizing individuals who are not contributing positively to your life.

Recognizing toxic individuals in your life is an essential step towards safeguarding your mental health. Once you've identified them, you can take proactive steps to establish boundaries, protect your peace, and manage your anxiety better.

Limiting Exposure to Toxic Individuals

Once you've recognized toxic individuals in your life, it's important to take steps to limit your exposure to them. Boundaries act as a mental and emotional fence, safeguarding your mental well-being and peace.

Consider limiting the time you spend with these individuals. This can mean cutting down on unnecessary interactions, spending less time in their company, or not engaging in lengthy conversations. It's vital to remember that your time and energy are precious resources, and you have the right to choose how you spend them.

Develop strategies to distance yourself emotionally, even when physical distance isn't possible. This could mean mentally preparing yourself before interactions, not taking their criticisms to heart, or practicing mindfulness techniques to maintain your emotional balance.

Avoid sharing personal or sensitive information that could be used against you. Toxic individuals may exploit vulnerabilities to manipulate or belittle you. Keeping such information to yourself can help protect your emotional health.

Dealing with Unavoidable Toxic Relationships

Sometimes, toxic individuals might be people you can't easily avoid, like family members or coworkers. In such cases, creating boundaries becomes even more crucial.

Establish clear communication rules, stating what you find acceptable and what you don't. This might feel uncomfortable initially, but it's essential for your mental health. If they disregard your boundaries, consider seeking help from a mediator, counselor, or HR representative.

Try to maintain emotional detachment during interactions. Viewing them as a detached observer, rather than an emotionally involved participant, can help minimize the impact of their toxicity.

Finally, practice self-care diligently. Engaging in activities that promote relaxation, positivity, and mental resilience can provide a buffer against the negative effects of unavoidable toxic relationships.

In conclusion, creating boundaries with toxic individuals, whether by limiting exposure or managing unavoidable relationships, can significantly reduce anxiety and stress. It empowers you to reclaim control over your emotional environment, paving the way for better mental health and inner peace.

When and How to Seek Professional Guidance

Recognizing when to seek professional help is crucial in managing anxiety and dealing with toxic individuals. There are several signs that indicate the need for professional guidance. For instance, if your anxiety becomes overwhelming, impedes daily activities, or if the situation with a toxic individual is causing you distress and you feel unable to cope.

Professional guidance can take many forms, from one-on-one counseling or psychotherapy, to medication, depending on the severity and nature of your anxiety. It's important to reach out to a trusted healthcare provider who can guide you towards the appropriate help. They can provide an initial assessment and referral to a mental health professional if needed.

Remember, reaching out for help is not a sign of weakness but a proactive step towards healing and growth. It can provide you with valuable tools and strategies to manage anxiety, cope with toxic relationships, and improve your overall mental health.

Therapy and Support Groups: Allies in your Journey

Therapy is a powerful ally in the journey towards mental health. Therapists, psychologists, or psychiatrists can provide different types of therapy like Cognitive-Behavioral Therapy (CBT), Dialectical Behavior Therapy (DBT), or EMDR (Eye Movement Desensitization and Reprocessing), among others, depending on your needs.

Therapy provides a safe and confidential environment where you can discuss your feelings, fears, and experiences. It can help you understand the roots of your anxiety, recognize unhelpful thought patterns, and develop coping mechanisms. Therapy can also assist in building assertiveness and boundary-setting skills, essential in dealing with toxic individuals.

Support groups, either online or in-person, are another valuable resource. They provide a sense of community and shared understanding, making you feel less alone in your experiences. Support groups offer a platform to share experiences, learn from others going through similar situations, and gain emotional support and encouragement.

In conclusion, professional help, be it therapy or support groups, can play a pivotal role in your journey towards managing anxiety and dealing with toxic relationships. They provide guidance, tools, and a supportive environment, empowering you to navigate your path towards mental health with increased confidence and resilience.

Attracting Uplifting and Supportive Relationships

Establishing uplifting and supportive relationships is a crucial step in cultivating positive influences and managing anxiety. These relationships act as a source of comfort, understanding, and positivity, providing a safe space for expression and mutual growth.

To attract such relationships, it's important to first understand your own worth. Recognize that you deserve respect, kindness, and understanding in your relationships. Be clear about the traits you value in others - such as empathy, positivity, respect, and honesty - and look for these in new acquaintances.

Strive to embody these qualities yourself. Like attracts like, and being a source of positivity and support can draw similar people towards you. Also, participating in social activities, clubs, or communities that align with your interests or values can increase the chances of meeting like-minded individuals.

Remember, building meaningful relationships takes time and patience, but the impact on your mental health and overall quality of life is well worth the effort.

Engaging in Positive Activities and Hobbies

Engaging in positive activities and hobbies that you enjoy can significantly contribute to managing anxiety and fostering a positive mindset. Such activities can serve as a source of joy, relaxation, and self-expression, acting as a counterbalance to the stressors of daily life.

Consider activities that promote mindfulness and relaxation, such as yoga, meditation, or nature walks. These can help reduce anxiety, improve mood, and foster a sense of inner peace.

Pursue hobbies that bring you joy and a sense of accomplishment. This could be anything from painting, reading, cooking, to gardening. Hobbies not only keep you engaged and occupied, but they also provide opportunities for personal growth and creativity.

Volunteering or contributing to a cause you care about can also be rewarding and uplifting. It provides a sense of purpose and connection, promoting positive emotions.

In conclusion, cultivating positive influences, through uplifting relationships and engaging activities, can greatly enhance your mental health and resilience. These positive influences act as pillars of support in your journey, helping to manage anxiety and fostering an environment conducive to growth and well-being.

The Cumulative Impact of Positive Changes

Making positive changes, even small ones, in your environment can have a significant cumulative impact on your mental health over time. These changes can influence your mood, thought patterns, and overall perspective on life, playing a vital role in managing anxiety.

Creating a positive physical environment, such as a tidy home or a peaceful workspace, can provide a sense of calm and order, reducing feelings of overwhelm. Filling your space with elements that inspire joy, like art, plants, or sentimental items, can boost positivity and well-being.

However, the concept of a positive environment goes beyond the physical. It also includes your social environment - the people you interact with. Surrounding yourself with supportive, uplifting individuals can enhance your self-esteem, resilience, and overall happiness.

Lastly, a positive digital environment is equally crucial in today's connected world. This involves curating your social media and news intake to limit negativity and ensure a balance of positive, inspiring content.

These individual changes, while seemingly small, can add up over time, creating a powerful shift towards a more positive, anxiety-manageable lifestyle.

Building Resilience against Anxiety through Positive Environments

A positive environment, physical, social, and digital, can significantly boost your resilience against anxiety. Resilience refers to your ability to cope with stress and adversity, and it can be nurtured and strengthened over time.

A serene physical environment provides a sense of security and calm, serving as a safe haven from external stressors. A supportive social environment enhances emotional resilience, providing a network of care and understanding that can buffer against anxiety. Lastly, a balanced digital environment can shield against information overload and the anxiety-inducing effects of negative news or social comparison.

Actively nurturing these positive environments and maintaining them can help build a strong foundation of resilience. This resilience not only equips you to better manage anxiety but also enhances your overall well-being and quality of life.

In conclusion, harnessing the power of a positive environment is a key strategy in managing anxiety. Through the cumulative impact of positive changes and the nurturing of resilience, a positive environment can serve as a strong ally in your journey towards better mental health.

Chapter 12 Harnessing the Power of Gratitude

The Science Behind Gratitude and Mental Health

Gratitude has been widely recognized in psychological research as a powerful tool for enhancing mental health. It involves acknowledging the good things in life – from the beauty of a sunset to acts of kindness, and recognizing their value.

Scientifically, practicing gratitude has been shown to trigger positive changes in the brain. Neuroimaging studies suggest that gratitude-related activities activate regions of the brain associated with social bonding, pleasure, and reward, and also those linked with decision-making and empathy. This brain activation pattern is part of why experiencing gratitude enhances feelings of satisfaction and happiness.

Furthermore, gratitude can boost the production of serotonin and dopamine – neurotransmitters responsible for feelings of happiness and well-being. This can help to combat depressive symptoms, which often co-occur with anxiety.

How Gratitude Alleviates Anxiety

Gratitude is a potent antidote to anxiety for several reasons. Firstly, by focusing on positive experiences, it helps shift attention away from worries and fears, thereby reducing the cognitive resources available for anxiety-provoking thoughts.

Gratitude also fosters a sense of abundance and contentment, countering the scarcity mindset often linked with anxiety – the feeling that we are lacking or that something bad is about to happen. By consciously acknowledging and appreciating the good in life, we can alleviate these fears and create a more balanced, realistic perspective.

Additionally, expressing gratitude can help to strengthen social relationships. Feeling connected and supported by others can reduce feelings of anxiety and enhance our ability to cope with stressors.

In conclusion, the power of gratitude lies in its ability to trigger positive brain changes, shift our focus from worries to positives, foster contentment, and strengthen social bonds, all of which contribute to alleviating anxiety.

Cultivating Mindful Awareness: Recognizing Moments of Gratitude

Developing a gratitude mindset begins with cultivating mindful awareness of the world around you. Being mindful involves being present and fully engaged in each moment, observing your surroundings and experiences without judgment.

To recognize moments of gratitude, practice tuning into small details – the warmth of sunlight streaming through your window, the aroma of freshly brewed coffee, a kind word from a friend, or a quiet moment of peace in a busy day. These moments, while easily overlooked, are opportunities for gratitude that can provide a profound sense of joy and contentment.

Meditation can be a helpful tool in developing this mindful awareness. Techniques like mindfulness meditation or loving-kindness meditation can enhance your ability to stay present and recognize positive experiences, paving the way for a more grateful mindset.

Shifting Perspective: Seeing the Good in Everyday Life

Seeing the good in everyday life requires a shift in perspective. It's about choosing to focus on positives rather than dwelling on negatives, recognizing blessings rather than burdens, and viewing challenges as opportunities for growth rather than obstacles.

For instance, instead of being frustrated by a delay in your morning commute, you might appreciate the extra time to listen to a favorite podcast. Instead of criticizing yourself for a mistake, you might thank yourself for the opportunity to learn and grow.

This shift in perspective isn't about denying or ignoring life's challenges, but about choosing a more balanced and positive lens through which to view them. It's a conscious decision to appreciate the good in each day, regardless of its challenges.

In conclusion, developing a gratitude mindset is a two-pronged process involving mindful awareness of the present moment and a perspective shift towards positivity. By cultivating these habits, you can unlock the abundant opportunities for gratitude in everyday life, fostering a more positive outlook and reducing anxiety.

Starting a Gratitude Journal: A Daily Ritual of Reflection

Keeping a gratitude journal can be a highly effective way to cultivate a sense of appreciation in your daily life. The practice is simple: each day, you write down things that you are thankful for. These can range from major events, like receiving a promotion at work, to small joys, like a delicious meal or a call with a loved one.

By documenting these moments, you actively shift your focus towards positive experiences, which can help to counterbalance the anxiety-inducing effects of negative events or thoughts. Moreover, seeing your blessings written out can offer a powerful visual reminder of the abundance in your life, even during challenging times.

Try to make your gratitude journaling a daily ritual. You could start or end your day with this practice, using it as a time of peaceful reflection. Remember, consistency is key in reaping the benefits of gratitude journaling.

Expressing Gratitude Towards Others: Strengthening Connections and Boosting Happiness

Expressing gratitude towards others is another practical way to cultivate appreciation. Not only does it affirm the positive aspects of your relationships, but it also strengthens your connections, fostering feelings of belonging and support.

You might express gratitude directly by thanking someone for their help or kindness. Or you could write a gratitude letter, detailing all the ways someone has positively impacted your life. Even silent acknowledgment of others' contributions to your well-being can enhance your sense of gratitude.

Expressing gratitude towards others does not just boost your happiness but also increases the well-being of the receiver, creating a positive feedback loop that enhances overall positivity and reduces anxiety.

In conclusion, practicing gratitude through a daily journal and expressing appreciation towards others are practical, impactful ways to foster a grateful mindset. These practices can serve as a daily reminder of the abundance in your life, counteracting anxiety and boosting overall well-being.

Gratitude as a Shield Against Negative Thoughts

Gratitude can act as a powerful shield against negative thoughts, which are a common contributor to anxiety. By focusing your attention on positive experiences and acknowledging the good in your life, gratitude can help to break the cycle of negative, worry-fueled thinking.

When you catch yourself slipping into negative thought patterns, intentionally shift your focus to something you're grateful for. This can act as a circuit breaker, disrupting the cycle of anxiety-inducing thoughts and replacing them with more positive, comforting ones.

It's important to note that practicing gratitude is not about denying or suppressing negative emotions. Instead, it's about creating a more balanced perspective, where positives are given as much recognition as negatives. This balanced perspective can serve as a protective shield, making you more resilient against stress and worry.

The Long-term Impact of a Gratitude Practice on Anxiety

The benefits of gratitude aren't just immediate; they're also long-term. Regularly practicing gratitude can lead to enduring changes in the way you perceive and interact with the world, which can have a profound impact on anxiety.

Over time, gratitude can help to retrain your brain to focus more on positives and less on negatives, reducing the frequency and intensity of worry-filled thought patterns. This can also foster a greater sense of peace and contentment, buffering against stress and anxiety.

Moreover, the social benefits of gratitude – such as enhanced relationships and feelings of connectedness – can provide a lasting source of support and positivity, further reducing anxiety.

In conclusion, the healing power of gratitude can be seen in its ability to shield against negative thoughts and its long-term impact on anxiety. By fostering a positive perspective and enhancing social bonds, a regular gratitude practice can act as a powerful tool in managing anxiety, boosting resilience, and enhancing well-being.

Thanking Yourself: Gratitude Towards Personal Growth and Achievements

Often, we tend to focus our gratitude outward, appreciating the people and circumstances that bring us joy. While this outward gratitude is beneficial, it's also important to direct gratitude inward, towards ourselves.

Practicing gratitude for your personal growth and achievements can boost self-compassion and self-esteem. Recognize the progress you've made, the challenges you've overcome, the skills you've developed, and the personal goals you've achieved. Even small victories, like successfully managing a difficult conversation, taking care of your health, or getting through a tough day, are worthy of gratitude.

Thanking yourself nurtures a kinder, more compassionate relationship with yourself. It encourages you to acknowledge your worth and strength, fostering a positive self-image that can help alleviate anxiety and self-doubt.

Being Grateful for Your Strengths: Building Confidence and Reducing Anxiety

Every individual possesses a unique set of strengths – qualities that contribute to their character and abilities. These might include kindness, creativity, determination, patience, or a knack for making people laugh. Taking the time to recognize and appreciate these strengths can boost confidence and reduce anxiety.

Make it a habit to reflect on your strengths and express gratitude for them. This not only reinforces a positive self-perception but also helps you to see yourself as capable and resilient, qualities that counteract feelings of helplessness often associated with anxiety.

Recognizing your strengths can also inspire you to utilize them more effectively, empowering you to manage challenges and stressors with greater confidence. This can create a positive feedback loop, where gratitude enhances self-efficacy, reduces anxiety, and inspires further growth and resilience.

In conclusion, incorporating self-compassion into your gratitude practice – through thanking yourself for personal growth and appreciating your strengths – can have a powerful impact on anxiety. It nurtures a positive self-image, boosts confidence, and promotes resilience, offering a strong foundation for managing anxiety and enhancing overall mental well-being.

Chapter 13 Eliminating Negative Thoughts in People with Anxiety

The Mechanisms of Negative Thinking

Negative thinking, also known as negative self-talk, refers to the mental dialogue you have with yourself that limits your ability to believe in yourself and your own abilities. These thoughts often distort your perception of experiences and events, making you see the worst in yourself, others, and situations.

This pattern of thinking isn't always based on facts but rather on internalized beliefs and expectations. For instance, you may think, "I'm bound to fail this test," even though you've adequately prepared and have a history of good performance. Negative thinking often involves cognitive distortions, such as overgeneralization, magnification (or catastrophizing), and binary thinking (viewing things in absolute, black-and-white terms).

Negative thoughts are often automatic, arising spontaneously in response to certain triggers. They are self-perpetuating, meaning one negative thought can trigger another, leading to a downward spiral of negativity.

The Link Between Negative Thoughts and Anxiety

Negative thinking and anxiety share a mutually reinforcing relationship. On one hand, habitual negative thinking can lead to and exacerbate anxiety. When you constantly anticipate the worst and underestimate your ability to handle situations, it naturally evokes feelings of anxiety and fear.

On the other hand, anxiety can also foster negative thinking. When you're anxious, your thought process tends to narrow down to focus on perceived threats or potential negative outcomes. This can bias you towards negative thinking, creating a vicious cycle where anxiety and negative thoughts feed off each other.

Negative thoughts play a key role in many anxiety disorders. For instance, in generalized anxiety disorder, individuals tend to have excessive worry about various aspects of their life, often anticipating the worst possible outcome. In social anxiety disorder, negative thoughts about one's social performance and fear of negative evaluation from others are common.

In conclusion, understanding the nature of negative thoughts and their connection to anxiety is the first step towards breaking the cycle of negativity. By gaining insight into these processes, you can start to recognize and challenge your negative thoughts, reducing their impact on your mental well-being.

Common Negative Thought Patterns

Negative thought patterns, also known as cognitive distortions, are irrational or exaggerated thoughts that distort our perception of reality. These patterns often arise automatically, are hard to recognize, and can greatly contribute to anxiety. Here are a few common ones:

1. **Catastrophizing**: This involves imagining and expecting the worst possible outcome in any situation. For example, you might immediately think you're going to be fired if you make a minor mistake at work.
2. **Overgeneralization**: Here, you draw a general rule or conclusion based on a single incident or piece of evidence. If something bad happens once, you expect it to happen over and over again.
3. **Black-and-White Thinking**: Also known as "all-or-nothing" thinking, this distortion involves viewing things as either good or bad, with no in-between. For example, you might think, "If I'm not perfect, I'm a failure."
4. **Mind Reading**: This involves assuming that you know what others are thinking, usually that they are thinking negatively about you.
5. **Fortune Telling**: You predict the future negatively without considering other, more likely outcomes.
6. **Labeling**: Instead of recognizing errors in specific behaviors, you assign negative and global labels to yourself or others based on perceived shortcomings.

Identifying Your Personal Thought Traps

To combat negative thinking, you first need to be aware of when and how it manifests in your own mind. Here are some strategies to identify your personal thought traps:

1. **Mindfulness**: Practice being present and observing your thoughts without judgment. This can help you notice when you're slipping into negative thought patterns.
2. **Thought Records**: Keep a journal of situations that cause you anxiety or distress. Note what happened, what you were thinking, how you felt, and any resulting behaviors. Over time, you'll start to see patterns in your negative thinking.
3. **Challenging Your Thoughts**: Whenever you catch yourself thinking negatively, ask yourself: "Is this thought based on facts or feelings? Is there another way to view the situation? How would I advise a friend in this situation?" This can help you identify and eventually change your distorted thought patterns.
4. **Seeking Professional Help**: Therapists and psychologists are trained to help you recognize and understand your patterns of negative thinking. Cognitive-behavioral therapy, in particular, can be highly effective in teaching you to identify and challenge cognitive distortions.

By recognizing these patterns of negative thinking and learning to identify them in your own thought process, you can begin to challenge and change your thoughts, leading to less anxiety and better mental wellbeing.

Cognitive Behavioral Techniques for Challenging Negative Thoughts

Cognitive Behavioral Therapy (CBT) is a therapeutic approach that helps you recognize and change dysfunctional thought patterns that lead to negative emotions and behaviors. Here are a few key CBT techniques for challenging negative thoughts:

1. **Thought Stopping**: When you notice a negative thought, mentally tell yourself "stop." This can serve as a kind of interrupt signal, breaking the chain of negative thinking.
2. **Cognitive Restructuring**: This involves identifying and disputing irrational thoughts. You learn to challenge the validity of the negative thought, and replace it with a more balanced and positive one.
3. **Evidence Gathering**: Write down the negative thought, then list the evidence that supports and contradicts it. Often, you'll find there's more evidence against the negative thought than for it.
4. **Decatastrophizing**: If you're prone to catastrophizing, this technique involves questioning the likelihood of the worst-case scenario and planning how you would cope if it did happen.

5. **Mindfulness and Acceptance**: Practicing mindfulness helps you stay in the present moment rather than dwelling on past regrets or worrying about the future. Acceptance involves acknowledging negative thoughts without judgment and letting them pass without engaging with them.

Implementing Socratic Questioning

Socratic questioning is a method used in cognitive therapy to challenge irrational or illogical thoughts. It involves asking yourself a series of questions about your negative thoughts to expose contradictions or unrealistic beliefs. Here are some examples of Socratic questioning:

1. **Clarification Questions**: "What does this thought mean? Can I explain it in simpler terms?"
2. **Probing Assumptions**: "What am I assuming that leads me to this thought? Are these assumptions valid?"
3. **Evidence Questions**: "What evidence do I have that this thought is true? What evidence do I have that it's not true?"
4. **Impact Questions**: "How does believing this thought affect me? What would change if I didn't believe it?"
5. **Alternative Perspective Questions**: "How might someone else view this situation? What's another way to interpret these events?"

These techniques can help you challenge negative thoughts and reduce their influence on your feelings and behavior. However, if you find these techniques challenging to implement on your own, consider seeking help from a mental health professional trained in CBT. They can guide you through these strategies in a structured and supportive environment.

The Power of Positive Affirmations

Positive affirmations are statements that can help you challenge and overcome negative thoughts and self-sabotaging patterns. They encourage positive changes in your life by influencing your subconscious mind, the part of your mind that influences your behavior, habits, beliefs, and emotions.

The key to effective positive affirmations is to make them personal, positive, and in the present tense. They should also be realistic and specific. For example, instead of saying, "I will not fail," you might say, "I have prepared for this task and I will do my best."

It's also beneficial to visualize yourself as you want to be while saying your affirmations, as this reinforces the message to your subconscious mind. Regular practice of positive affirmations can help in creating a more optimistic mindset and combating negative thoughts.

Techniques for Positive Reframing

Positive reframing doesn't mean ignoring or denying negative events. Instead, it means trying to see things in a different, more optimistic light, especially in situations that cannot be changed. Here are some techniques:

1. **Find the Silver Lining**: Try to find some positive aspects in every situation, no matter how small or insignificant they might seem at first.
2. **Practice Gratitude**: Focus on the things you are grateful for. This can help shift your focus from negative aspects to more positive ones.
3. **Choose Positive Language**: The language you use shapes your perceptions. Try to use more positive language in your daily life and notice how it changes your perspective.
4. **Cultivate Optimism**: Practice expecting the best outcome in every situation. This does not mean you should ignore potential risks or pitfalls, but rather balance a realistic view with positive expectations.
5. **Adopt a Growth Mindset**: See challenges as opportunities for learning and growth rather than as threats. This mindset can help you approach difficulties with a more positive attitude.

Remember, these strategies may not always be easy to implement, especially if you're in the habit of negative thinking. However, with practice and persistence, they can help you replace negative thoughts with a more positive, balanced perspective, thereby reducing anxiety.

Mindfulness: Being Present with Your Thoughts

Mindfulness involves paying attention to your experiences in the present moment in a non-judgmental way. This includes your thoughts, feelings, and physical sensations. Practicing mindfulness can help you become more aware of your negative thought patterns as they arise, which is the first step in learning to manage them.

You can practice mindfulness through formal meditation practices, like seated mindfulness meditation or mindful movement practices like yoga. But you can also incorporate mindfulness into your daily life in simple ways. For instance, you might practice mindful eating, paying close attention to the taste, texture, and smell of your food, or you could practice mindful walking, focusing on the sensation of your feet touching the ground.

Mindfulness is not about getting rid of negative thoughts, but rather about learning to observe them without getting caught up in them. This can help you realize that thoughts are just thoughts – they're not facts, and they don't control you.

Acceptance: Allowing Negative Thoughts to Pass

Acceptance, in the context of managing negative thoughts, involves acknowledging your thoughts and feelings without trying to change or suppress them. This might sound counterintuitive, but struggling against negative thoughts can often amplify them and create additional stress.

Imagine your thoughts as cars passing by while you're standing on the side of the road. You can observe each car as it passes, but you don't need to chase after them. Similarly, you can learn to observe your negative thoughts as they arise and then let them go, without getting swept up in their narrative.

Acceptance does not mean resignation or complacency. Instead, it's about giving yourself permission to have negative thoughts and understanding that they are a normal part of the human experience. This approach can help to reduce their power over you and make them easier to manage.

Practices like mindfulness and acceptance are skills that take time to develop. It can be helpful to work with a mental health professional or take part in a mindfulness-based stress reduction program. However, even a few minutes of mindfulness practice each day can go a long way towards helping you manage negative thoughts and reduce anxiety.

Recognizing and Halting Negative Thought Spirals

Negative thought spirals, also known as rumination, occur when you get caught up in a cycle of negative thinking. These spirals can often feel overwhelming and uncontrollable. Recognizing when you're caught in a negative thought spiral is the first step towards halting it. Here are a few signs that you might be in a thought spiral:

- You're constantly thinking about past failures or future problems.
- Your thoughts are repetitive and difficult to control.
- You're feeling more anxious or depressed the more you think about a particular topic.

Once you've recognized that you're in a negative thought spiral, you can use various strategies to halt it:

1. **Mindfulness**: As discussed earlier, mindfulness can help you observe your thoughts without getting caught up in them.
2. **Distraction**: Engage in a task that requires your full attention. This can help break the cycle of negative thinking.
3. **Physical Activity**: Exercise can have immediate benefits for your mood and can help disrupt a negative thought spiral.
4. **Self-Compassion**: Speak to yourself as you would to a friend in distress. Acknowledge that it's okay to feel the

way you do, and that you're capable of overcoming challenges.

Building Resilience against Negative Thought Spirals

Building resilience against negative thought spirals involves cultivating habits that promote positive thinking and emotional wellbeing. Here are a few strategies:

1. **Maintain a Regular Sleep Schedule**: Lack of sleep can exacerbate negative thinking. Prioritizing good sleep hygiene can help.
2. **Healthy Nutrition**: A healthy diet can contribute to better mood regulation and overall mental wellbeing.
3. **Regular Exercise**: Physical activity can help reduce anxiety and improve mood, making you less susceptible to negative thought spirals.
4. **Social Connection**: Spending time with supportive friends and family can help you feel more grounded and less susceptible to negative thinking.
5. **Mental Health Support**: Consider seeking help from a mental health professional if negative thought spirals are affecting your quality of life. Cognitive-behavioral therapy, in particular, can be very effective in addressing this issue.

Remember, everyone experiences negative thoughts from time to time. It's a part of being human. However, if negative thought spirals become frequent or unmanageable, it may be a sign of an underlying mental health condition, and it's important to seek professional help.

When to Seek Professional Help

It's important to remember that everyone experiences negative thoughts, and having them doesn't necessarily mean that you need professional help. However, if your negative thoughts are persistent, causing significant distress, impacting your daily life, or leading to feelings of hopelessness or suicidal thoughts, it's time to reach out to a professional.

Other signs that you might benefit from professional help include:

- If your anxiety is leading to physical symptoms such as headaches, stomachaches, or a racing heart.
- If you're using substances like alcohol or drugs to cope with your thoughts or anxiety.
- If you're avoiding certain situations, places, or people due to anxiety.
- If your worries seem uncontrollable and are consuming a lot of your time.

Therapies for Addressing Negative Thoughts (CBT, ACT, etc.)

Several types of therapy can be effective for managing negative thoughts:

1. **Cognitive Behavioral Therapy (CBT)**: CBT is a common type of talk therapy that helps you become aware of inaccurate or negative thinking and respond to challenging situations more clearly and effectively. It's widely considered the gold standard treatment for anxiety disorders.

2. **Acceptance and Commitment Therapy (ACT)**: ACT involves learning to accept your thoughts and feelings rather than trying to reject or change them. The goal is to develop flexibility in how you respond to anxiety and negative thoughts.

3. **Mindfulness-Based Cognitive Therapy (MBCT)**: MBCT combines mindfulness techniques like meditation and breathing exercises with elements from cognitive therapy. It's designed to help you become more aware of your thoughts and feelings and to respond to them in a non-judgmental way.

4. **Dialectical Behavior Therapy (DBT)**: DBT is a form of CBT that emphasizes the development of skills like mindfulness, emotional regulation, and interpersonal effectiveness. It's particularly effective for those who struggle with emotional dysregulation or self-harming behaviors.

It's crucial to remember that seeking professional help is a sign of strength, not weakness. Mental health professionals are trained to help you understand and navigate your feelings, develop coping strategies, and lead a satisfying, anxiety-free life. If you're unsure where to start, your primary care doctor can often provide an initial assessment and referral to a mental health professional if needed.

Chapter 14 Resources

Navigating anxiety can be challenging, but you don't have to do it alone. A wealth of resources is available to provide guidance, support, and relief. Here, you'll find an array of resources tailored to the needs of those living with anxiety in the U.S., from self-help books and reputable online platforms to crisis hotlines.

Books

These books offer practical strategies for managing anxiety and cultivating gratitude. They are grounded in evidence-based practices and personal experiences, providing both expert insights and relatable narratives.

1. "The Anxiety and Phobia Workbook" by Edmund J. Bourne: A comprehensive guide offering practical strategies to cope with and overcome anxiety.
2. "Feeling Good: The New Mood Therapy" by David D. Burns: Provides Cognitive Behavioral Therapy-based techniques to challenge and alter negative thought patterns.
3. "The Upward Spiral" by Alex Korb: Offers a neuroscience-based approach to managing depression and anxiety.

4. "Thanks!: How Practicing Gratitude Can Make You Happier" by Robert Emmons: A helpful guide in understanding the science and art of gratitude practice.

5. "The Gratitude Diaries: How a Year Looking on the Bright Side Can Transform Your Life" by Janice Kaplan: A year-long exploration of the author's personal journey practicing gratitude.

Online Resources

These reputable websites offer advice, resources, and community support for those living with anxiety.

1. Anxiety and Depression Association of America (ADAA) (www.adaa.org): Provides extensive resources, including educational materials, personal stories, blogs, webinars, and a therapist directory.

2. National Institute of Mental Health (NIMH) (www.nimh.nih.gov): Offers a wealth of information about anxiety and other mental health conditions, as well as links to clinical trials and resources in Spanish.

3. Mental Health America (www.mhanational.org): Provides a broad array of resources on mental health, including online screenings for anxiety and other mental health conditions.

4. Mindful (www.mindful.org): Offers advice and practices for mindfulness and meditation, which can be beneficial tools for managing anxiety.

5. Psychology Today (www.psychologytoday.com): Offers
    articles on a wide range of mental health topics, and a
    comprehensive directory of therapists, psychiatrists,
    therapy groups, and treatment centers.

Emergency and Crisis Hotlines

If you find yourself in a crisis, these hotlines provide
immediate, confidential support.

1. National Suicide Prevention Lifeline: Call 1-800-273-
    TALK (8255), or use the online Lifeline Crisis Chat
    (www.suicidepreventionlifeline.org).
2. Crisis Text Line: Text HOME to 741741 to connect with
    a crisis counselor.
3. Substance Abuse and Mental Health Services
    Administration's (SAMHSA's) Disaster Distress
    Helpline: Call 1-800-985-5990 or text TalkWithUs to
    66746.

Remember, while these resources provide valuable information
and immediate support, they are not a substitute for
professional medical advice or treatment. Always reach out to
healthcare professionals if you're struggling with anxiety. You
are not alone, and help is available.